D

t he   r before

Sportsmanship

Nick Hunter

www.raintreepublishers.co.uk
Visit our website to find out
more information about
Raintree books.

To order:
☎ Phone 0845 6044371
🖹 Fax +44 (0) 1865 312263
🖥 Email myorders@raintreepublishers.co.uk

Customers from outside the UK please telephone +44 1865 312262

Raintree is an imprint of Capstone Global Library
Limited, a company incorporated in England and Wales
having its registered office at 7 Pilgrim Street, London,
EC4V 6LB – Registered company number: 6695582

Edited by Adrian Vigliano and Claire Throp
Designed by Richard Parker
Picture research by Ruth Blair
Originated by Capstone Global Library Ltd
Printed and bound in China by Leo Paper Products Ltd

ISBN 978 1 406 23475 6
15 14 13 12 11
10 9 8 7 6 5 4 3 2 1

British Library Cataloguing in Publication Data
Hunter, Nick
Sportsmanship. – (Ethics of sport)
175-dc22
A full catalogue record for this book is available from
the British Library.

Acknowledgements
We would like to thank the following for permission
to reproduce photographs: Alamy pp. 10 (© Ace Stock
Limited), 47 (© Niall McDiarmid); Corbis pp. 9, 12,
24, 29, 33 (© Bettmann), 16 (© Philippe Lecoeur/
MAXPPP/epa),17 (© Juice Images), 19 (© Laci Perenyi/
dpa), 30 (© John A. Angelillo), 40 (© Jason Edwards/
National Geographic Society), 45 (© Leo Mason),
51 (© Victor Fraile), 53 (© BPI); Getty Images pp. 7
(Hulton Archive), 8 (Nick Laham), 15 (Bob Thomas),
21 (Brian Bahr), 22 (Julian Finney), 25 (Tom Shaw),
27 (Christopher Lee), 34 (J. Meric), 36 (Laurent
Fievet/AFP), 37 (Rich Frishman/Sports Illustrated),
39 (German Alegria/MLS), 42 (Popperfoto), 49 (Cyril
Folliot/AFP); Shutterstock pp. 4 (© Benis Arapovic), 23
(© Eoghan McNally), 50 (© photogolfer).

Cover photograph of tennis players shaking hands
reproduced with permission of Getty Images (David
Madison/Stone).

We would like to thank Shawn E. Klein for his
invaluable help in the preparation of this book.

Every effort has been made to contact copyright holders
of any material reproduced in this book. Any omissions
will be rectified in subsequent printings if notice is
given to the publisher.

Disclaimer
All the Internet addresses (URLs) given in this book
were valid at the time of going to press. However, due to
the dynamic nature of the Internet, some addresses may
have changed, or sites may have changed or ceased to
exist since publication. While the author and publisher
regret any inconvenience this may cause readers, no
responsibility for any such changes can be accepted by
either the author or the publisher.

CONTENTS

Sportsmanship and ethics...4

What is sportsmanship?...6

Fair play in history 10

Rules 16

Respect...24

Pressure to succeed 36

Sportsmanship and culture 40

Sportsmanship and you 46

Does sportsmanship matter? 50

Topics for discussion...54

Glossary 56

Notes on sources 58

Find out more 61

Index..64

Some words are printed in bold, **like this**. You can find out what they mean by looking in the glossary.

SPORTSMANSHIP AND ETHICS

It's the biggest football match of the season. Two sides battle it out to be the best, roared on by a huge crowd and many more people watching at home. Tensions run high, as the two sides know that one mistake could hand the title to their opponent, while one moment of skill or luck could lead to being crowned champions. Suddenly, a goal is scored from nowhere. Everyone celebrates wildly. There are only a few seconds to go, and the home team has won the game!

However, in the minutes that follow, television replays show that the ball went out of play before the goal was scored. The losing team and its fans cannot believe that the official missed it. In an interview, the player who scored the winning goal talks about "a lucky break" and shrugs his shoulders. Did he know the ball had gone out, but played on anyway? "It's up to the official to enforce the rules," he replies.

When you play sport with your friends, there is no official to enforce the rules. Players have to do the right thing.

Doing the right thing

In another close contest in a championship tennis match, a player serves, needing one point to win the match. Her second serve is called out, giving the opposing player a point and a chance to get back into the match. But the opposing player is not happy. She is talking to the umpire and saying that the serve was actually a good one. The server should have won the point and the match. The umpire changes the decision. The player's honesty has handed the game to her opponent.

How would you have reacted in these two situations? Would you have claimed victory when you knew the ball had gone out of play without being seen by the official? Or would you have admitted that the official had got the decision wrong, even if that meant you lost the game? You may never have to make a decision like this in an important game. But when we play sport, we often have to make decisions about what is the right thing to do.

Ethical questions

When we have to make a decision about what is the right thing to do, we call this an **ethical** question. In sport, as in other areas of life, the laws of the game answer some questions. The player in the first example could claim that the official should decide when a rule has been broken.

However, there are plenty of examples when the right choice is about acting in the spirit of the game, rather than just following the rules. In the second example, the tennis player saw that an incorrect decision had been made. She acted in the right way to make sure the correct player won the game – even if this changed the umpire's decision. Doing the right thing in sport is called **sportsmanship**.

"The true athlete should have good character, not be a character."[1]

John Wooden, former UCLA basketball coach and winner of 10 National Collegiate Athletic Association (NCAA) championships

WHAT IS SPORTSMANSHIP?

You probably have an idea of what sportsmanship means to you. You might be able to think of an example from your favourite sport of someone showing great sportsmanship. You can probably also think of examples when an athlete showed bad sportsmanship. This book will look at many examples of good and bad sportsmanship, as well as the ethical questions that we all face in sport. But before we can consider these questions, we need to decide what we mean by sportsmanship.

Rules and regulations

Sportsmanship is not just about following the rules of the game. Following the rules is a basic requirement for playing any sport. Having said this, as we will see, not all the rules of a game are exactly equal. Some are essential for the game to work, while others are less essential to making a game run smoothly. Although sportsmanship is not just about following the rules, the two can go together. A player who tries to get away with breaking rules may be guilty of bad sportsmanship.

The right spirit

Showing good sportsmanship, or being a good sport, is more about the spirit in which the game is played. A good sport can be contrasted with someone who tries to "win at all costs". Sportsmanship is about recognizing that playing the game fairly and in the right spirit is at least as important as winning. This does not mean that a good sport does not want to win. Rather, a good sport just wants to win fairly. Many of the examples of good sportsmanship in this book were performed by some of the greatest figures in their different sports.

> "The ethical behaviour exhibited by a sportsman or athlete . . . generally considered to involve participation for the pleasure of a fair and hard-fought contest, refusal to take unfair advantage of a situation or of an opponent, courtesy towards one's opponent, and **graciousness** in both winning and losing."[1]
>
> Definition of sportsmanship from *Webster's Sports Dictionary*

Some instances of sportsmanship are obvious examples of people doing the right thing. But there are also many cases that are not quite so clear. Because the rules of sportsmanship are not written down, what one person thinks is good or bad sportsmanship another person might think is quite normal behaviour.

BARON DE COUBERTIN (1863–1937)

Baron Pierre de Coubertin was a French nobleman and educator. His inspiration to found the modern Olympic Games came from watching sport being played in British and US schools and colleges. In the 1800s, the idea that sport was good for people was not widely recognized. De Coubertin saw that sports – played in the right way – could not just have health benefits, but could also help people to develop ideas of fair play and teamwork.[2]

"What is important in life is not victory but the battle. What matters is not to have won, but to have fought well."[3]

Baron Pierre de Coubertin, speaking during the London Olympic Games in 1908. These Games were hurt by accusations of bad sportsmanship between British and US athletes and officials.

Kinds of sportsmanship

The more we try to define "sportsmanship", the clearer it becomes that good sportsmanship takes many different forms, as does bad sportsmanship. Those who behave in a sportsmanlike way may demonstrate many different qualities.

Honesty

One kind of sportsmanlike behaviour is honesty. Honest athletes are happy to admit when they have broken a rule. Often they have broken a rule by accident. Many athletes are prepared to admit to a mistake, even if it gives the advantage to their opponents. But there are also many examples of athletes who have not shown such honesty, possibly because they do not want to let their teammates down.

One aspect of honesty is being honest about one's own performance. This becomes apparent when people act like good winners and good losers. We have all seen examples of managers and players being interviewed after losing a game and claiming that they lost because of a decision by a referee or umpire, or because of a bit of bad luck. In many cases, this may be true. But how often do you see the same people say that they only won because of a lucky break? Good sports recognize that the dividing line between the two is narrow. They are gracious when they win, but they also accept the result when they lose.

Sportsmanship is about accepting decisions from officials, whether you agree with them or not.

GOLD MEDAL FOR SPORTSMANSHIP

US athlete Mildred "Babe" Didrikson was one of the greatest athletes of the 20th century. She played many different sports at the highest level, including track and field, basketball, and golf. At the 1932 Olympics, Didrikson won gold medals in the javelin and 80-metre hurdles.

Didrikson may have been successful, but she was seen as obnoxious and **arrogant** by many of her fellow athletes. They begged US athlete Jean Shiley to defeat Didrikson in the high jump. The two jumpers managed to jump the same height, but Didrikson's final jump was ruled illegal, and Shiley was awarded the gold medal. Far from enjoying the defeat of her fellow athlete, Shiley offered to have the gold medal cut in half, so that Didrikson could get the share that Shiley felt she deserved.[4]

Jean Shiley was gracious in victory at the 1932 Olympics.

Enjoying sport

Other kinds of sportsmanship include helping others and generally playing sports with a smile and sense of enjoyment. This is the opposite of the tough **professional** who believes that winning is the only reward worth having. Even some of the toughest players, who love nothing better than winning, show honesty and respect for their fellow athletes.

"If you can meet with triumph and disaster and treat those two impostors just the same."[5]

From the poem *If* by Rudyard Kipling. These words are written above the entrance to Centre Court at the Wimbledon tennis grounds.

FAIR PLAY IN HISTORY

You might think that the debate about sportsmanship is new. However, questions about sportsmanship have been asked for as long as sport has been played, just as questions about honour and doing the right thing have been part of all societies in the past.

Ancient Greece

The first organized sporting event that we know about in detail was the ancient Olympic Games, first held at Olympia, Greece, around 776 BC. For the ancient Greeks, sporting events were closely linked to religion and peace. Still, the contests between athletes from city-states such as Athens and Sparta were as fierce as any of today's international sporting rivalries. Every four years, a "sacred **truce**" was declared so that the games could take place. Athletes were free to travel and compete without being attacked by enemies from other states. Although this sacred truce protected the athletes, many of the rivalries between city-states were played out on the Olympic stage.

The ancient Olympic Games included "heavy" events such as wrestling (shown here) and boxing. These were more violent than the modern versions of these sports but they still had rules. Wrestlers were allowed to trip their opponents but punching and eye-gouging were not allowed.

Winning was everything for these athletes. Victorious athletes became huge celebrities, while defeated athletes were said to slink home as quietly as possible. Although they may not have shared the modern view that taking part is more important than winning, the ancient Greeks made sure that everyone knew about any athletes found guilty of **bribery**, lying, or cheating. These athletes were fined, and the money was used to create statues of the Greek god Zeus called *zanes*. These *zanes* lined the entrance to the Olympic stadium, reminding athletes of the consequences of doing the wrong thing.[1]

Gladiators of ancient Rome

Sport in ancient Rome was brutal. Fights between gladiators, or between gladiators and wild animals, in arenas such as the Roman Colosseum usually ended in death for someone. Despite the bloodthirsty nature of Roman sport, even the Romans had some idea about sportsmanship.

Priscus and Verus were two of the greatest gladiators. They fought an epic battle to mark the opening of the Colosseum. The fight was so ferocious and so long that, eventually, both gladiators are said to have held up their fingers at the same time, to admit defeat. Emperor Titus, who in most fights would signal whether a defeated gladiator should live or die, declared them both winners and granted them their freedom. For once, the fight itself was more important than who won or lost.[2]

MEDIEVAL CHIVALRY

If our modern idea of sportsmanship has a direct ancestor, it may be the **medieval** code of **chivalry**. Medieval chivalry was the code of honour and courtesy followed by knights, both in war and in everyday life. While there was very little organized sport in medieval Europe, the sport that existed was linked to war, such as jousting between knights and archery as practice for soldiers. The rules of chivalry extended to these sports. Eventually, chivalry came to mean simply courtesy, particularly between men and women.

Development of modern sport

The first sports as we know them today began to develop in the late 1700s and 1800s. Some of these sports had been played for many years. One of the main things that changed in the 1800s was that rules for different sports began to become standard. Before that, there were many different versions of rules played at, for example, different schools. The rules of "association football" (known as football or soccer) were standardized in England in 1863.[3] Baseball, the oldest distinctly US sport, began to spread around 1850.[4]

WILLIAM GILBERT (W. G.) GRACE (1848–1915)

W. G. Grace was one of the first sporting superstars. He played cricket for the Gloucestershire and England teams and was an important figure in the development of the game. Grace was also renowned for bending the rules. One of his friends remarked that, "his **gamesmanship** added to the fund of stories about him" — and his opponents said much worse than that. Once, when an umpire said he was out, Grace complained, "They came to see me bat, not you umpire." On another occasion, the ball became caught in his clothing. He continued running while fielders tried to get it back.

Many of these new sports grew in private high schools and colleges. The people who ran these schools began to believe that playing sport could have **moral** benefits as well as health benefits for young people. They believed that sport could teach young men – as athletes usually were men at this time – to be leaders and to develop an understanding of right and wrong. So, as sports became organized, ideas of sportsmanship began to develop too.

The amateur ideal

The development of sportsmanship in the 1800s was also closely tied to the ideal of the **amateur** athlete. As sports began to spread from schools and rules were standardized, professional **leagues** began to develop. Many people felt that sportsmanship was not possible in professional sport, in which athletes are paid. Amateur athletes – who are unpaid and play sport for the love of it – were seen as the true examples of sportsmanship.

Amateurism was an important part of the Olympic Games. Professional athletes were not allowed to compete in the Games until the late 20th century[6], but this wasn't always fair. Jim Thorpe won gold medals in the pentathlon and decathlon at the Stockholm Olympics in 1912. Later, the remarkable Thorpe was stripped of his medals. What was his crime? He had earned a few dollars playing baseball, making him a professional. Thorpe's medals were later restored, but long after he had died. Sometimes, sports governing bodies are as guilty as athletes of doing the wrong thing.[7]

Over time, sports that had mostly originated in Britain, the United States, and France began to grow and spread around the world. As these sports spread, ideas of sportsmanship began to circulate with them. At their worst, sports such as cricket were promoted in **colonial** empires of countries such as Britain as a way for local people to learn about the values and culture of their colonial rulers. However, in many cases, sports took root and lasted longer than the empires that brought them. The 20th century saw sports develop as a symbol of national pride and culture.

"You may as well praise a man for not robbing a bank."[8]

US golfer Robert Tyre Jones, Jr, responds to praise for his sportsmanship. Jones lost the US Open by one shot in 1925, after telling officials he had hit his ball twice, which led to a one-shot penalty.

The modern era

During the 20th century, sports such as rugby, baseball, basketball, tennis, and especially football spread around the world. Teams formed leagues in many countries, and those countries competed against one another in global events such as the football World Cup and the Olympic Games. As sport became global, it also became big business. Spectators paid to watch sport in huge stadiums or even on television. At the start of the century, a popular sports team may have attracted fans from the local area. Today, those fans could be anywhere in the country – or even on the other side of the world – thanks to widespread **media** coverage.

Growth of professionalism

The growth of professional sport has brought big rewards to the very best athletes. They earn big money and are cheered by thousands of fans. However, this has brought new pressures, as there are huge sums of money riding on whether they win or lose. Although most people who play sport are still amateurs playing purely for enjoyment, athletes competing at the top level are professional and are paid according to results. Some people think this means that sportsmanship itself is under pressure.

National pride

Another feature of sport in the modern era has been the growth of competitions between different nations. The world's biggest sporting nations want to be at the top of the medals table at the Olympics. This and other international contests can lead to bitter rivalries, such as the one between the United States and the **Soviet Union** during the years of the **cold war**. These nations brought their military rivalry into the sporting arena. Sport became a substitute for military conflict – with little room left for sportsmanship.

"Serious sport has nothing to do with fair play. It is bound up with hatred, jealousy, boastfulness, disregard of all rules and **sadistic** pleasure in witnessing violence: in other words it is war minus the shooting."[9]

Author George Orwell, "The Sporting Spirit", 1945

Although some national rivalries can be bitter, others are built on mutual respect and often feature displays of sportsmanship (see box below).

SHARING THE RYDER CUP

Sportsmanship has always been important in the sport of golf. One of the best examples happened in the Ryder Cup of 1969. The Ryder Cup is played between a team from Europe (in 1969 this team was made up of Britain and Ireland) and a team from the United States. These two teams play a series of matches.

US golfer Jack Nicklaus, the best player in the world at the time, and Britain's best player, Tony Jacklin, were on the final green of the last match of the tournament. Jacklin had to make a 2-foot putt. If he missed, the United States would win the Ryder Cup. If he holed the putt, the two teams would be tied. Nicklaus conceded, meaning that he assumed that Jacklin would hole the putt, so he did not need to take the shot. Nicklaus' words summed up his respect for his opponent: "I didn't think you were going to miss that one, but I didn't want to give you the opportunity."[10]

RULES

All sports have rules. Some sports have so few written rules that every player knows them without being told. Other sports have a thick book of rules built up and refined over many years. In addition to the official rules of the sport, there are often unofficial rules and customs that have grown over time. You cannot read these unofficial rules, but you learn them by playing.

Rules are rules?

Breaking the rules of a game is not allowed. It can also be seen as bad sportsmanship – although this is not always the case.

For example, in football, an attacking player is not allowed to be closer to the goal than the last defender when the ball is passed to him or her. This is called offside. But someone who breaks this rule is not considered a bad sport. Many attacking players try to play as close as possible to being offside. Sometimes they might score a goal by being just offside, and this is seen as part of the game. Opposing fans and players don't complain that the player was offside. They blame the referee for not spotting it.

Thierry Henry was one of the world's best footballers. When he handled the ball while scoring to prevent Ireland from reaching the World Cup, it damaged the reputation of this great player for many people.

STEALING SIGNS

Baseball is one game in which many unwritten rules and customs have developed over time. Ideas of sportsmanship depend on observing these rules as much as the official ones. During the game, the catcher signals to the pitcher to indicate what the next pitch (or throw) should be. If the opposing batter can "read" these signals, he or she can gain an advantage. It is not illegal for a batter to read or "steal" these signals. When batters have been accused of stealing signs, they usually deny it – although many players admit that everyone does it. However, it is seen as unsportsmanlike to get an advantage by understanding the code between the catcher and pitcher.[1]

However, if the same player, rather than being offside, controlled the ball with his or her hand, the player would be accused of cheating. This was the case with the French striker Thierry Henry, who did this in a crucial game against Ireland in 2010.

As these examples show, the rules of the game may be clear, but the reality of playing a sport is not always clear-cut. Both the examples given here are against the rules, but players and fans see them differently. This proves that the rules of the game are not really designed to deal with the spirit of the game. It is here – in the spirit of the game – that questions about sportsmanship truly come into play.

Unwritten rules

What is considered cheating or bad sportsmanship may change over time, even if the rules don't change. Some rules carry a greater moral weight than others. An example of this might be a custom in professional cycling. It is understood that cyclists should not take advantage of a mechanical problem experienced by an opponent. But in 2010, Spanish cyclist Alberto Contador was accused of taking advantage of a problem with the chain on the bike of his chief rival, Andy Schleck. Contador claimed not to have known about Schleck's mechanical failure. Breaking this unwritten rule was seen by many fans and fellow cyclists as more serious than breaking the written rules of the sport.[2]

Using the rules to your advantage

An athlete can sometimes break the written rules of a sport without being seen to break the code of sporting behaviour. There are also plenty of examples when sportspeople play within the rules but could be accused of being unsportsmanlike. Some people would argue that rules are there to be challenged as long as athletes accept that they will be penalized if they break the rules.

Sometimes foul play itself is within the rules. "Personal fouls" in basketball include holding, blocking, or pushing an opponent. Fouls are allowed – but there are consequences. Committing a foul means that the team will surrender possession or give a free throw to the opposition. If an individual player commits six fouls, he or she must leave the game. The team also has a limited number of total personal fouls. After it hits this mark, free throws are given away for all subsequent fouls.[3]

It makes sense for some personal fouls to be allowable, as they are often very minor. However, teams may choose to purposefully foul to prevent the opposition from scoring.

A question of intent

Those who have a strict idea of sportsmanship would argue that any kind of deliberate foul is unacceptable, as it goes against the spirit of the game. These people would argue that whether something is fair play or not depends on the intentions of the athlete committing the foul. If the athlete commits a foul to get an advantage, then this is unsportsmanlike behaviour. This is one reason why questions of sportsmanship are so **controversial**. Fans and officials cannot always know whether a foul was intentional or not.

FAIR OR FOUL IN FORMULA ONE?

German driver Michael Schumacher dominated the sport of Formula One motor racing in the 1990s and 2000s. He was a talented driver, but many of his opponents felt the force of his will to win, which often went up to and beyond what was allowed under the rules. For example, the Adelaide Grand Prix in 1994 was the last race of the season. Schumacher would become world champion if his rival, Damon Hill, did not finish ahead of him. While trying to stay ahead of Hill, Schumacher's car was damaged when it slid into a wall. Knowing that he would not win the race with a damaged car, Schumacher appeared to steer his damaged car into Hill's path. Both drivers were out of the race, and Schumacher was crowned world champion.[4]

In high-speed crashes such as the one between Schumacher and Hill, more is at stake than just fair play. Drivers risk serious injury or even death.

Enforcing the rules

Often the most controversial figures in a sporting contest are the people who must enforce the rules. When their team loses, fans and coaches will often blame a decision on the referee or umpire. This can be easier than admitting that they lost to worthy winners. Of course, officials sometimes make mistakes, as do players and coaches. But every decision they make is examined and questioned, particularly in high-profile televised sports.

The referee's job is to make sure that players follow the rules. This seems fairly clear, but even here the referee's role is open to different views. Some players and coaches argue that the presence of the referee means that players have no responsibility to respect the rules or admit when they have broken the rules. If a rule is broken, it is the job of the officials to spot it. Others would argue that sportsmanship requires players to observe the rules, rather than relying on the referee.

The Corinthian spirit

The Corinthians football team provides an extreme example of this view. The Corinthians, an amateur team based in London, were at their strongest in the years before World War I (1914–18), when professional football was becoming popular. Their overseas tours did much to spread football around the world. The team Real Madrid later adopted the Corinthians' famous white shirts as their own.

The Corinthians had a strict moral code of how they believed the game should be played. They were known to correct referees who gave incorrect decisions in their favour. It is said that, if a penalty kick were awarded to them for deliberate foul play by another team, the Corinthians would deliberately not score. They believed that no player could be so unsportsmanlike as to deliberately foul another, so they would not accept the penalty. If the Corinthians' code of fair play meant that they did not obey the referee, they were prepared to do so.[5]

Questioning referees

The example of the Corinthians is so extreme that it seems comical when compared to modern sport. Respect for officials varies in different sports, but many people believe that, in some sports, respect for referees has declined in the modern era. It is difficult to know if this is true.

The actions of professional players are seen by millions of fans. Does this affect young players' views of what sportsmanlike behaviour is?

The growth of live televised sport means that incorrect decisions are highlighted more than ever before. In some sports, controversial moments are shown on big screens in the venue during the game, so players, spectators, and officials can see when a mistake has been made. This undoubtedly causes more questioning of decisions.

SCHOOL SPORT

Respect for referees is a concern at many levels of sport. Many people believe that bad behaviour towards officials in professional leagues sets a bad example for athletes at **grassroots** levels, including in schools. For example, in 2010 a high school basketball player in Florida attacked a referee after the referee penalized him for shoving another player. The player pushed the referee and then threw him to the ground.[6]

Technology and respect for officials

Until recently, referees did not have the benefit of seeing replays before making difficult decisions. They had to make decisions instantly, based on what they could see at the time. Critics of the referee's decision may have had the benefit of seeing lots of different camera angles and slow-motion replays before concluding that the official had got it wrong.

In many sports, technology is helping to change this. The question is: Does using technology support the officials on the field and encourage good relationships between officials and players?

Many sports have helped officials by using technology. Tennis and cricket both use "hawkeye" systems that can track the movement of a ball to see where it has bounced. Players are allowed to review decisions by the officials – although there is a limit on how many reviews they can make if they turn out to be incorrect. Although players are questioning the umpire's authority, this has reduced the conflict between players and officials, as all sides are prepared to accept the results of technology.

SERENA WILLIAMS CROSSES THE LINE

Using technology to help officials provides no guarantees that players will not abuse them. In 2009 US tennis star Serena Williams was fined £51,400 for verbal abuse of a line judge, who had called her for a fault at a crucial point in a match. Although she later apologized, Williams' initial reaction was an angry one: "An apology from me? How many people yell at linespeople? I see it happening all the time. I don't know how many times I have seen that happen."[7] It is natural for athletes to base their actions on what they see others do, but it is no defence for unsportsmanlike behaviour.

Two sports that have resisted calls to use technology are football and baseball. Football's world governing body, the International Federation of Association Football (FIFA), has also rejected the use of technology for disputed goals, saying that it would undermine officials on the field.[8] Many in baseball feel that using instant replays to decide close decisions would make the game last too long.[9] Those who are in favour of technology argue that officials' decisions would be strengthened if technology means that more decisions are correct.

Technology and sportsmanship

Technology may mean that more decisions are correct, and so it might improve relations between players, coaches, and officials. But does it lead to better sportsmanship? Is technology so important because players cannot be trusted to be honest? And does technology put too much pressure on referees?

Rugby is a tough sport. Many players admit that in the past, punches were often thrown in tight situations. This was against the rules, but it was rarely spotted and was considered normal. Technology such as replays and rules being applied more strictly means that this happens much less often in modern rugby.[10]

RESPECT

Although respect for rules and officials is an important part of sportsmanship, an even bigger issue is how athletes choose to behave.

Respect for other athletes

Perhaps the central issue in being a good sport is having respect for the other players. After all, a game in the park may not have a referee, but for the game to work, players have to be honest and show respect for one another. How do athletes show respect for other players? This applies to opponents as much as teammates. It means treating everyone fairly during the game and not trying to get an unfair advantage. Of course, there are many views on what an unfair advantage is, and we will look at examples of behaviour that you may think falls into this category over the next few pages.

Win at all costs

Some people, such as the baseball legend Ty Cobb (see box below), might argue that winning is the only thing that matters. There are many coaches and athletes at all levels of sport who would agree with this. There are also plenty of examples of winners who have not forgotten the importance of winning fairly and showing respect for their fellow athletes. However, the belief that winning is everything puts sportsmanship under pressure in many ways.

TY COBB (1896–1961)

Ty Cobb, known as the "Georgia Peach", was one of baseball's greatest players. However, he is just as well-known for his fierce will to win, and there are many stories of his attempts to **intimidate** opponents. Cobb once said, "Baseball is something like a war,"[1] and he played as if he believed it, making enemies wherever he went. There were stories that Cobb sharpened his spikes so he could injure opponents when he slid into a base. He later denied this, but he believed that stories like this gave him an edge over his opponents.[2]

RESPECT BETWEEN RIVALS

In 2005, the teams from England and Australia played one of the most exciting series of matches ever seen in cricket. Although the cricket was hard-fought, one image summed up the great respect between these two sides. At the end of a test match that England won by the tiny margin of one run, England's Andrew Flintoff took time to **commiserate** with Australia's Brett Lee, one of his beaten opponents, before celebrating with his own teammates. Flintoff understood that the contributions of both teams to a great game were more important than the victory itself. This seemed to sum up the idea of sportsmanship.

Diving and faking injury

One way that players show questionable conduct is by pretending to be injured. This is particularly common in football, where "diving" has become widespread in the professional game. There have also been examples of players acting as if they have been fouled in basketball, known as "flopping". American football players have also been known to pretend to be injured in order to slow down the game.

Faking a foul or injury shows a lack of respect to other players for two reasons. Anyone doing it is seeking to gain an advantage by pretending that a rule has been broken. These athletes are also claiming that another player has deliberately fouled them and, in extreme cases, this may lead to innocent players getting penalized or sent off.

How diving works

One of the most worrying things about diving in football is that it has become an accepted part of the game. A player will be tackled and will fall to the ground, possibly rolling over a couple of times to make sure the referee doesn't miss the dive. This is particularly likely to happen if the player is in an area of the field where a penalty or free kick might lead to a goal. Everyone involved knows that the player is trying to mislead the referee. But no one is offended by such an action – everyone knows that it happens all the time. Sometimes players who are guilty of diving will even try to get an opposing player sent off as a result of their deception.

Faking it

Diving has become so widespread in football that examples of players not diving are celebrated. In 1997, Liverpool player Robbie Fowler was awarded a penalty. Fowler jumped up, saying that he had in fact tripped and that it was not a penalty. What many people forget about this example of sportsmanship is that the referee gave the penalty kick anyway. Fowler took it and, although his kick was weak, another Liverpool player scored on the rebound. What most people remember, however, is the honesty that Fowler showed in saying he had tripped.[3]

In September 2010, Tampa Bay Rays pitcher Chad Qualls pitched to Yankees player Derek Jeter. As the ball moved towards him, Jeter grabbed his elbow as though in pain. The umpire sent Jeter to first base, because he was hit by the ball. Replays later showed that the ball did not actually hit Jeter. He faked the whole thing. He was called "Jeter Cheater", by some fans, but Jeter said, "What am I supposed to say [to the umpire]? 'Sorry sir, but it didn't hit me, please let me continue to hit?'"[4]

RUGBY'S "BLOODGATE" SCANDAL

In 2009, rugby union was hit by a major scandal when it was revealed that several people worked to mislead officials. Tom Williams, a player for London's Harlequins, was brought onto the field by his coach, Dean Richards. Williams took a blood capsule that had been bought from a local joke shop. He bit into the capsule, pretending that he had a blood injury. This allowed another player to be reintroduced – something that was only allowed if a player were injured.

It later emerged that this form of cheating had happened before. This time it was uncovered – even though a team doctor cut Williams' lip to create a real injury. Despite attempts by the other people involved to make Williams take all the blame himself, many of those involved were handed long bans as a result.[5]

While the injury in this photograph was real, the "bloodgate" scandal shocked the rugby world. It involved more than just Tom Williams (above) and coach Dean Richards. Medical staff and club officials were also involved in the deception.

"Sledging"

Another way that athletes may try to get an advantage over their opponents is using **psychology**. This is rarely covered by the rules, and it happens in many sports. It could occur when a coach or manager mischievously suggests that a rival team may not have the mental toughness to win. It can also take the form of personal or even **racist** abuse directed at an opposing player by players or spectators.

Verbally abusing, or "**sledging**", opponents has become a part of many sports. What do athletes hope to achieve by this? It is said that, at the top level, a big part of the secret to sporting success is in the mind. Getting "under the skin" of the opposing players could be an important step to winning if it breaks their concentration or undermines their confidence.

Although this kind of verbal abuse can be seen as bad sportsmanship, this is not necessarily the case if both sides take part willingly and the comments do not cause offence. If everyone is taking part, then it could be argued that no one is gaining an unfair advantage. However, "sledging" can become less pleasant if certain opponents are singled out for some reason.

"TRASH TALKING" IN BOXING

Boxing is one of the toughest of all sports. While violence is considered the ultimate act of bad sportsmanship in many sports, it is the whole point of boxing – although within strict rules. The sport also thrives on verbal abuse between boxers prior to a fight. This is designed to build anticipation of the fight and to gain the upper hand mentally. Do you think this verbal abuse is unsportsmanlike, or is it acceptable because it has become part of the sport?

Violence on the field

Some of the worst cases of bad sportsmanship happen when a desire to win spills over into violence. This can be the case particularly in contact sports such as rugby and American football, in which players are involved in a hard physical battle. The worst examples include tackles that are planned to injure and remove a player from the game. This goes against all concepts of sportsmanship.

Muhammad Ali was possibly the greatest boxer of all time. He traded insults with his opponents as much as any boxer, but he also had a strong sense of doing the right thing.

"I don't care about looking good to fans. I want to look good to God. I got to sleep good at night. And how am I going to sleep if I kill a man . . . just to satisfy you writers?"[6]

Boxer Muhammad Ali responds to critics saying that he did not try hard enough to knock out a weaker opponent

Drugs and cheating

There are many examples of unsportsmanlike behaviour when athletes have been disrespectful to their fellow athletes. Many of these actions are visible to everyone on the pitch or in the stadium. However, some examples of athletes cheating their fellow athletes are hidden.

Performance-enhancing drugs are a major problem in many sports, particularly in sports such as track and field, which depend on strength and speed. **Steroids** are drugs that can build muscles to artificially increase an athlete's strength. Performance-enhancing drugs are illegal in almost all sports. Athletes who take them have to live a double life, lying to friends and fellow athletes.

During his career, Barry Bonds hit more home runs than any other Major League Baseball player. However, this record has been overshadowed by persistent allegations and evidence of steroid use by Bonds and many others in the sport.

When you hear of an athlete being caught taking drugs, do you think of this as unsportsmanlike behaviour? If not, think about how this affects other athletes. First of all, the athlete taking drugs is trying to get an unfair advantage. If the athlete wins a medal, he or she may be denying that medal to a "clean" athlete, and this could damage that athlete's career or ability to earn money. It can also affect how spectators view all the athletes in a sport. If we know that some athletes are using drugs, we will question every amazing performance. All athletes are damaged by the use of drugs.

"Everybody else is doing it"

Athletes who use drugs and their supporters would argue that drug use is so widespread that they are at a disadvantage by *not* taking drugs. Some also claim that coaches encourage them to use drugs, implying that this is quite normal. However, there are many great athletes who have won without using drugs and who have taken a stand against those who would cheat their way to a gold medal.

TAINTED GOLD

Winning Olympic gold is the ultimate achievement of any athlete's career. The record books show that the great US sprinter Michael Johnson won four Olympic gold medals between 1992 and 2000. Johnson was actually awarded five Olympic gold medals, but in 2008 he decided to return the medal he won as part of the US 4x400-metre relay team at the Sydney Olympics in 2000. Johnson made this decision when he discovered that Antonio Pettigrew, his friend and teammate, had admitted to using performance-enhancing drugs at that time. Although Johnson had not known about Pettigrew's drug use until many years later, he felt that the medal had been won unfairly.[7]

"I know that the medal was not fairly won and that it is dirty, and so I have moved it from the location where I have always kept my medals because it doesn't belong there. And it doesn't belong to me. So, as difficult as it is, I will be returning it to the International Olympic Committee because I don't want it. I feel cheated, betrayed, and let down."[8]

Michael Johnson explains his reasons for returning the Olympic gold medal he won in Sydney

Not trying your best

When we watch or play sport, we have to believe that the players we are watching or playing against are playing at the highest level they are capable of. If athletes do not try their best, it shows a real lack of respect for opponents and for people who have paid to watch the game.

There are many reasons why athletes might be tempted not to try their best. Sometimes money is the motive. There have been examples in many sports of players or officials receiving illegal payments not to perform.

In a team game, players may not perform because of a dispute with teammates or because they plan to move to another team. In this case, a player who is not trying his or her best is cheating teammates.

Tennis star Andre Agassi admitted in his autobiography, *Open*, that he had deliberately lost or "tanked" matches, including the semi-final of the Australian Open, for personal reasons. You might think that Agassi was cheating no one but himself. But what about the spectators who had paid a lot of money to cheer him on, or his opponent, Michael Chang, who now knows that he reached the Australian Open final because his opponent wasn't trying? He may have won anyway, but he will never be totally sure.[9]

SPORTSMANSHIP IN "SPORTS ENTERTAINMENT"

In extreme cases, when the action and result of a game are fixed, it is no longer a sport. Professional wrestling is very popular in many countries. Professional wrestling, which should not be confused with the Olympic sport of wrestling, describes itself as "sports entertainment",[10] and wrestling matches are designed to build characters and stories of heroes and villains. Wrestlers are there to play their role. The sportsmanship of good wrestlers and the apparently unsportsmanlike behaviour of the villains are all part of the story.

JOHN LANDY (1930–)

In 2002 a statue called "Sportsmanship" was unveiled in Melbourne, Australia. The figure chosen to represent sportsmanship was Australian middle-distance runner John Landy (shirt number 156 in the photo). In a championship race in 1956, Landy's fellow Australian athlete Ron Clarke tripped and fell. Landy tried to avoid him, but his running spikes caught Clarke's arm. Landy stopped, checked that his rival was okay, and helped him to his feet. He then continued the race and won it, finishing a few seconds outside the world record.

In later years, Landy admitted to being embarrassed by the praise he received for his act of "senseless chivalry", as one newspaper described it. "I think sport is about winning and about records . . ." he said. "This was a very personal business and I think it's unfortunate that such a lot is made of it."[11]

For the right reasons

There are some situations when not trying can be the right thing to do. US athlete Jimmy Connors was probably the best male tennis player of the 1970s. Connors' reputation was as an aggressive and sometimes controversial competitor. In the Australian Open final of 1975, Connors had benefited from several incorrect decisions against local favourite John Newcombe. As the crowd started to complain, Connors deliberately served a double fault, which gave a point back to his opponent. What Connors had not expected was that, after his little act of sportsmanship, Newcombe would go on to win the championship.[12]

Role models

Whenever athletes behave badly, on or off the field, spectators and the media ask what kind of example they are setting for young people. Do we have any right to expect athletes to set an example just because they are well paid and famous? Even if we expect athletes to behave on the field of play, are we entitled to expect good behaviour elsewhere in their lives?

Lessons in life

Lessons about how to behave come from many different people, particularly our parents, but also from other people who have an influence on our lives, such as friends and teachers. If we are athletes and sports fans, we are likely to follow the behaviour of well-known athletes in our chosen sport. If we see sporting heroes and heroines such as Serena Williams arguing with an official or an opponent, it may make us think that this kind of behaviour is acceptable. We may even think that this behaviour shows something about their winning mentality and is a reason behind their success.

Many people feel that unsporting behaviour on the field of play, such as arguing with officials, leads young athletes to believe that this kind of conduct is an accepted part of sport.

Should athletes be role models?

You could argue that top sports stars are role models whether they like it or not. Because their talent has helped to make them rich and famous, they have a duty to set an example about how to behave for those who follow them. Many athletes accept this role, devoting time and money to charities and supporting their community.

Those who oppose this view of athletes as role models would argue that we do not expect people in other well-paid professions to act as role models. There is no equivalent of sportsmanship for bankers, film stars, or business leaders. Although many of these people may behave like role models, it is not expected in the same way that it is of athletes.

Moreover, top sports stars are often young men and women who have suddenly started earning huge amounts of money and, in many cases, come from tough backgrounds and have missed out on part of their education through playing sport. It is difficult enough for them to manage the changes in their own lives, without having to worry about acting as role models for the rest of us.

"I'm not paid to be a role model. I'm paid to wreak havoc on the basketball court."[13]

Charles Barkley, former National Basketball Association (NBA) star

"Charles . . . I don't think it's your decision to make. We don't choose to be role models, we are chosen. Our only choice is whether to be a good role model or a bad one."[14]

Karl Malone, former NBA star, responding to Barkley

Who are your role models?

Do the actions of your favourite sporting heroes affect your own behaviour? You may want to be like the biggest football or basketball stars, with money, fame, and talent, but do your favourite stars also have qualities that you admire? Do they use their fame and money to help others? Do they play fair and impress people with the way they play as well as their skill? Should we expect millionaire sports stars to show us how to behave?

PRESSURE TO SUCCEED

We have seen that good and bad sportsmanship comes in many forms. But what are the reasons why athletes act as they do, and why do some behave differently from others? Professional athletes face many different pressures in their careers, and this can sometimes affect how they react in situations in which they have a choice between doing the wrong or the right thing.

Win at all costs

Many people play sport purely for enjoyment, but there is usually an element of competitiveness. Whether playing tennis against a friend or representing one's country at the Olympic Games, people want to win and prove they are better than their opponent. Anyone who plays competitive sport feels that pressure. When people are representing their school, college, university, or country, the pressure to win becomes even stronger. Sportsmanship requires athletes, often at a key point in a game or competition, to forget that competitive impulse and recognize that fair play is more important.

Although all athletes want to win, even the best have to accept defeat sometimes. True champions are remembered for being gracious in victory and defeat.

HOME-RUN HEROINES

Sara Tucholsky had never hit a home run before, so no one was more surprised than she was when she hit the ball out of the park in a college softball game between her Western Oregon team and Central Washington in 2008. To claim her home run, all Tucholsky had to do was a slow run around the bases. As she approached first base, she fell to the ground with a knee ligament injury. Her teammates were not allowed to help her, and it looked like that first home run would not happen after all. That was until Mallory Holtman and Liz Wallace, two members of the opposing team, offered to carry Tucholsky around the bases to complete the run. This act of sportsmanship cost Central Washington the game, but it will be remembered long after the result is forgotten.[1]

The cost of losing

In professional sport, competitive pressure is often increased or distorted by money. For a professional athlete, their sport earns them a living. Winning matters even more because it means the difference between success and failure – a new contract could be riding on the result. A player's actions may not just cost him or her money, but it could also affect teammates. Pressures like this can mean that professional athletes' focus on winning can sometimes override thoughts about fair play.

> "Show me a good loser and I'll show you a loser."
>
> Many people are said to have been the source of this quote, including American football coach Vince Lombardi

Is it really the case that an athlete who wants to win cannot be gracious and show sportsmanship in defeat? There are plenty of great winners who would dispute this. They may not have enjoyed losing, but they also recognized that fair play was just as important as winning.

Pressure from others

For many athletes, the pressure to win above everything else does not just come from the pressure they put on themselves. There are all sorts of outside pressures on athletes, from teammates and coaches to fans and the media.

Teammates and coaches can place pressure on athletes to act in the interest of the team – even if those interests go against sportsmanship. Many of the examples of sportsmanship in this book are from individual athletes in sports such as track and field, tennis, and golf. As with members of team sports, the careers of these athletes depend on whether they win. But, unlike members of team sports, they don't have to ask anyone's permission, and they can't be dropped by the coach.

Sportsmanship and spectators

Winning is also important to spectators and fans. Where team athletes might play for a number of different teams during their careers, fans are normally loyal to one team. This means that they become fiercely supportive of the actions of "their" players. On the other hand, their **bias** might lead them to apply different standards to other teams and players. An action that would be entirely justified from their own team might not be welcomed if a player on the opposition does the same thing. This biased attitude does not necessarily lend itself to an appreciation of sportsmanship. Of course, there are many fans of all sports who can support their own favourites while recognizing the importance of fair play and respecting their opponents.

Some of the most biased fans are often those supporting national teams. Sometimes their bias boils over with booing of national anthems and opposing players and, in some cases, racist abuse. Most supporters accept that these attitudes have no place in sport. Sportsmanship is as important in crowd behaviour as it is on the field of play.

Watching sport

When was the last time you watched a sporting event, live or on television? Think about whether you showed sportsmanship while watching the game. If your team or favourite sports star lost, did you blame it on the referee or some piece of bad luck? How did you react to decisions that went against your team or player? We all have our favourites, and it is natural to have a different reaction depending on whether something favours your side or not. But we can't expect athletes to be sportsmanlike if we, as fans, don't do the same.

David Beckham is sent off for foul play while playing for LA Galaxy in 2009. In 1998 Beckham was sent off while playing an important game for England against Argentina in the World Cup. He was heavily criticized by media and supporters. He later apologized for his actions and won over supporters with his positive reaction to the incident.

SPORTSMANSHIP AND CULTURE

Different sports, societies, and countries often have different ideas about what sportsmanship means. Even within one sport or country, different people have different ideas about sportsmanship. As we have seen, the rules of sportsmanship are never written down in the same way as the rules of sports.

Sports such as football are played in streets and open spaces around the world. Players have to develop their own ideas of sportsmanship and what is allowed.

These **cultural** differences can cause problems. What would be seen as clever tactics in some cultures becomes gamesmanship or cheating in others. In many of today's global sports, national teams play one another regularly. Players of different nationalities also play in major leagues across the world, such as the major football leagues in Europe and the US basketball and baseball leagues. Players from different countries bring different ideas.

Sportsmanship around the world

Players and coaches from around the world have brought many benefits to football in the United Kingdom, including a better understanding of diet and training. But many people say that diving to earn a foul was rare when most players on British teams were from Britain and Ireland. On the other hand, many of the crunching tackles that were common in football at that time would be seen as unacceptably violent in other parts of the world. Has the global nature of sports such as football meant that some cultural differences, including the details of sportsmanship, have been lost?

Although there are different ideas about the details of sportsmanship, there is a basic concept of the right way to behave towards a fellow athlete that crosses national and sports boundaries. Sometimes these values are put to the test in the real world.

FROM ALEXANDRIA TO JAPAN

Japanese athlete Yasuhiro Yamashita arrived at the Olympics in 1984 having not lost a judo match for seven years. Everyone expected him to win the gold medal – at least until he tore a muscle in his right leg in the early stages of the competition. Yamashita, despite being in pain and walking with a limp, made it to the final, where he faced Egyptian athlete Muhammad Ali Rashwan, a construction worker from Alexandria. Yamashita won the match.

Later, Rashwan said that he had deliberately not attacked Yamashita's bad leg, as it was against his **principles**. Although television pictures showed this was only partly true, Rashwan's sportsmanship appealed to the Japanese sense of honour. He became an unlikely star in Japan, prompting lots of interest in the culture of Islam.[1]

"Fair play is a great conception. In these two words are summed up all that English education and **ethics** hold most dear . . . Fair play means regard for one's neighbour and seeing the man and fellow player in one's opponent."[2]

Spoken by a German visitor to London in 1920. He also said that fair play was "untranslatable" and that many languages including French and Japanese do not translate the phrase.[3] His point was not that the English were the only people who practise fair play, but rather that the idea varied slightly in different countries and cultures.

Politics and sportsmanship

Politics have often entered the world of sport. When this happens, ideas of sportsmanship can be put to the most severe test. Perhaps the best example of this took place at the 1936 Olympic Games in Berlin, Germany.

Luz Long sets an example

The Berlin Olympics were to be Adolf Hitler's Games. The German leader saw the Olympics as the perfect opportunity to prove his idea that **Aryan** German people were superior to other races of people. Hitler's plan backfired when African-American sprinter and long jumper Jesse Owens claimed four gold medals.

Jesse Owens' opponent Luz Long was the first person to congratulate Owens when he won gold. Owens later wrote that: "You can melt down all the medals and cups I have, and they wouldn't be a plating on the 24-carat friendship I felt for Luz Long at that moment."[4]

Owens owed much of the credit for his victory in the long jump to Luz Long, a blonde-haired, blue-eyed model of Hitler's ideal German athlete. As Owens was struggling to qualify for the final, he talked with Long, who did not support Hitler's racist ideas. After two foul jumps in which he had overstepped the mark for a fair jump, Owens had one more chance to make the final. Long told him to jump from further behind the mark. Even jumping from further back than the other athletes, Owens would be good enough to qualify. Owens went on to beat his German friend in a closely contested final. Long was the first person to congratulate him – under the disapproving glare of Hitler.[5]

Mixing sport and politics

Politics and sport have been mixed many times since 1936. Athletes have had many opportunities to demonstrate sportsmanlike behaviour, even when faced with political situations that tried to create divisions between athletes. Many people say that sport and politics should not be mixed. But many athletes have felt that there are some situations where they have to take a stand.

STANDING UP FOR BELIEFS

Sportsmanship is about doing the right thing no matter what the circumstances. The gymnast Vera Caslavska had been involved in a pro **democracy** campaign in her **communist** home country of Czechoslovakia. Shortly before she was due to compete at the Mexico City Olympics in 1968, the **Soviet** army crushed this movement.

At the Olympics, many of the judges were from countries dominated by the Soviet Union. After some highly political judging, Caslavska had to share a gold medal with a Soviet athlete. As the two athletes stood on the podium and the Soviet national anthem was played, Caslavska deliberately turned her head aside, in protest against the invasion of her country. This was her only protest. But for this small act, Caslavska was denied the chance to compete or travel out of her country for many years.[6]

In the 1970s and 1980s, the sports community **boycotted** South Africa. This was in response to the country's policy of apartheid, which kept black and white people separate and unequal – in sport and in everyday life. The black majority had few rights compared to the white minority. The success of the boycott shows that the values of fair play and sportsmanship can have meaning outside sport, too.

The death of sportsmanship

Sumo wrestling is a very ancient sport, dating back at least 2,000 years. As the national sport of Japan, it has always been seen as a very traditional sport, with a strict code of honour. In 2011 several sumo wrestlers admitted to "fixing", or planning, the results of matches.[7] This was the latest scandal to hit the sport, after stories of illegal gambling and trainee wrestlers being mistreated. If such an ancient and supposedly honourable sport as sumo wrestling could face these scandals, what hope is there for the survival of sportsmanship elsewhere?

Media commentators and others often claim that sportsmanship is dead. They look back to a long-ago time when everyone played fairly and sportsmanship was always more important than winning. These people then point to the many examples of bad behaviour and scandals in modern sports, and they suggest that these examples show the death of sportsmanship.

Was there a golden age?

However, such an age of sportsmanship probably never existed. The modern Olympic Games, which began in 1896, have often been marred by outrageous examples of cheating. For example, at the 1904 St. Louis Olympics in the United States, Fred Lorz of the United States was congratulated by US president Theodore Roosevelt and almost awarded the gold medal for the marathon – until it was revealed that he had taken a ride in a lorry for part of the way.[8] It is also worth remembering that historically sport was often badly affected by **prejudice** based on race, gender, and class. Although this has not totally disappeared, it is less of a problem than it was in the past.

New and different pressures?

We are probably more aware of scandals and bad behaviour now because of the massive media coverage of athletes' lives on and off the field. This is just one of the pressures that affect today's professional athletes much more than those of the past. The rewards for winning are much greater than they have ever been before. This means that the costs of losing are greater than before, too.

FRIENDSHIP ACROSS THE NET

For most of us, sport is played with or against friends for the enjoyment of playing. The world of professional sport is often very different, but sometimes we can see the enjoyment of sport that most of us experience.

In the first round at the tennis tournament Wimbledon in 2008, the Swiss champion Roger Federer was playing Dominik Hrbatý of Slovakia. It was expected to be an easy win for Federer, and it was proving to be so. As the players changed ends towards the end of the match, Hrbatý asked Federer if they could sit together during the changeover, rather than on opposite sides of the umpire's chair, as usually happens. The two friends spent the break talking and laughing. This small incident showed that there was still room for friendship and respect between athletes, even during one of the world's biggest tournaments.[9]

SPORTSMANSHIP AND YOU

For much of this book, we have concentrated on sportsmanship in professional sports. But sportsmanship is not just about respect between athletes we see on television. It affects all of us who play sport. The values we learn playing sport, such as fair play and teamwork, are also important for the way we live our lives away from sport.

Attitudes to sportsmanship

Most athletes learn their first attitudes towards sportsmanship in school and club sports. This applies to top professionals as much as it does to anyone else.

Surveys of school athletes in the United States have found that, while many students recognize the importance of sportsmanship, this is not universal. More than a third of boys and almost half of American football players said it was more important to win than to be thought of as a good sport. Only 15 per cent of girls thought this was the case. Around 4 out of 10 boys and 3 out of 10 girls admitted that they had cheated or bent the rules at least once.[1]

The athletes were also asked specific questions, such as whether it was acceptable to fake an injury to buy their team some time. More than a third of boys and one in every five girls thought this would be acceptable.[2] Do you think you would find similar attitudes towards sportsmanship in your school or local sports club?

Despite these figures, most pupils in the survey thought that fair play was an important part of sport.[3] Respecting other people on the sports field is just as important as respecting them in other areas of life. If we expect others to treat us fairly, we need to be prepared to do the same ourselves.

HIGH SCHOOL HONOUR

Cleveland Stroud was coach of the Rockdale County High School basketball team, in Georgia, USA. In 1987 the team won the Georgia boys' championship for the first time, a great achievement for the school.

After the trophy had been awarded, Stroud noticed that the school had accidentally allowed an ineligible player, who had not passed enough classes, to play in one of the team's games. (In many US school sports, athletes have to pass a certain number of classes to be eligible for the sports team.) Stroud had no hesitation: A rule had been broken, and the trophy would have to be returned. Although this was difficult for all involved, the local community was immensely proud of the honesty the school had shown.[4]

"I told my team that people forget the scores of basketball games; they don't ever forget what you're made of."[5]

High-school basketball coach Cleveland Stroud

Sportsmanship is an issue for adults just as much as it is for young people.

47

Sportsmanship and everyday life

One of the reasons why sportsmanship is important for all of us is because these skills transfer to our everyday lives. We all have to obey rules in life, whether they are about not cheating on tests or getting to school or work on time. We don't always have a referee checking when we do the right thing.

Sportsmanship is partly about following rules like this, but it is more about following principles. Sometimes these principles are tested in extreme conditions, as in Pete Goss' rescue of Raphael Dinelli (see box on the next page). More often, however, these principles are tested in everyday situations – for example, when we have to decide whether it is right to lie about something, or to be disloyal to a friend.

Bad sportsmanship in real life

Think about some of the examples of bad sportsmanship you have read about in this book or seen for yourself. What do you think would happen if people constantly argued with police officers, as some athletes do with referees? What would happen if people dived to the ground and demanded compensation every time someone walked past them on the street? Many of the things that we call bad sportsmanship in sport would have serious consequences if they happened outside the sports arena.

Of course, the values of fair play and honesty are not just learned on the sports field. In fact, the survey discussed on page 46 found that athletes were slightly more likely to have cheated on a test than non-athletes.[6]

Values for life

In life we have to deal with many of the same things we encounter in sport. Having a sense of sportsmanship helps us to deal with defeats and setbacks graciously. It also helps us to be modest about our successes, recognizing that they are rarely achieved without help from others. Having a sense of fair play and the importance of working as a team help us to build strong relationships off the sports field, just as they do on the field.

LIFESAVER!

Occasionally, sportsmanship can mean the difference between life and death. British yachtsman Pete Goss (above) risked everything to rescue Frenchman Raphael Dinelli during the 1996 Vendée Globe around-the-world yacht race. During a ferocious storm in the Southern Ocean, Goss received a distress signal. Dinelli's boat was sinking. Goss would have to abandon his dream of winning the race to go to Dinelli's rescue, risking his own life in the process. He battled for two days through mountainous seas to reach the Frenchman, who had managed to survive in a life raft. After a detour to take Dinelli to Tasmania, Australia, Goss rejoined the race. He was one of only six boats to finish of the sixteen that started the race. Two competitors lost their lives in one of the most gruelling of all sporting contests.[7]

DOES SPORTSMANSHIP MATTER?

It is easy to say that we support the values represented by sportsmanship. After all, it is difficult to disagree with ideas such as fair play and honesty. If everyone took a brutal win-at-all-costs approach, sport would not be much fun to play or watch. Although we could never dismiss sportsmanship as a bad thing, does it really have a place in modern professional sport?

The trouble with sportsmanship

As we have seen, sportsmanship often means different things to different people. Can it really be any use if different countries and sports can't really agree on what it means? It is very easy to accuse someone of being a bad loser or taking an unfair advantage. But, in many cases, it can be difficult to prove. It also depends on a person's point of view.

During the 2000 Solheim Cup, the women's equivalent of the Ryder Cup, Swedish golfer Annika Sörenstam accused the US team of bad sportsmanship. The US team had forced her to replay a shot after accidentally playing out of turn. Under the rules of golf, the US team was correct. As with so many examples of good and bad sportsmanship, people's views of the issue depended on which team they were supporting.

Many athletes in modern sport are highly paid professionals. The decisions they make on the field can have big effects on their own careers, but also on the businesses they work for. Is it fair to ask them to make decisions based on an unwritten code of ethics? In other professions where people are expected to follow a code of ethics, this is usually clearly written down.

Sports do, of course, have a written code that athletes are supposed to follow. They are called the rules, and every sport has them. In addition to the rules of a sport, many tournaments and leagues have additional rules and guidelines. Those who think that sportsmanship is no longer relevant in modern sport would argue that any rules about how a sport should be played should be written down and clarified.

OUT-OF-DATE AT THE OLYMPICS?

Jamaican sprinter Usain Bolt was a big star of the Beijing Olympics in 2008. Bolt's record-breaking wins in the 100- and 200-metre races showed an athlete enjoying the pure thrill of running very fast. The whole world was captivated by Bolt's winning personality – or *almost* the whole world.

Jacques Rogge, the president of the International Olympic Committee, thought Bolt's celebration as he crossed the line to win the 100 metres was not very sportsmanlike. Rogge said: "I think he should show more respect for his competitors and shake hands, give a tap on the shoulder to the other ones immediately after the finish and not make gestures like the one he made in the 100 metres." Even some of sportsmanship's biggest supporters thought Rogge was taking things a bit far.[1]

The case for sportsmanship

For all the articles and commentators talking about the death of sportsmanship, it is difficult to imagine sport being played without any sense of sportsmanlike behaviour. For every professional athlete who plays only to win and make money, there are hundreds of others, both amateur and professional, who believe that the most important thing about sport is "not to have won, but to have fought well", as Olympics founder Pierre de Coubertin once said. They also believe that for sport to be worthwhile, it should be played with respect for the other people involved, whether they are players, officials, or spectators.

Those who think that sportsmanship is an outdated idea say that professional athletes do not need an ethical code to do their jobs. It is important to remember that, no matter how much top sports stars may earn, they are primarily there for entertainment. For the most part, sports fans want to be entertained by athletes who play fairly. If spectators could only expect to see cheating, violence, and bad sportsmanship, they would soon find somewhere else to get their entertainment.

DOING THE RIGHT THING

Darius McNeal stepped up to take the two free throws that his team, DeKalb High School, had been awarded for a technical foul. The first throw bounced in front of him and rolled a couple of feet. The second was even worse. DeKalb's opponents, from Milwaukee Madison High School, applauded the throws. Everyone knew that McNeal had missed on purpose.

That afternoon, Milwaukee player Johntel Franklin's mother had died. Franklin and friends had been at her bedside, but they wanted the game to go ahead. When Franklin arrived halfway through the game and asked to play, his team had to give up two free throws because his name wasn't on the team list. DeKalb tried to get the referee to ignore the free throws, but the referee refused. Still, sportsmanship demanded that they deliberately miss the free throws. Milwaukee went on to win the match, but McNeal and his teammates had done the right thing.[2]

Sport is never just about winning.

Sport for fun

The same holds true outside professional sport, where millions of people play sport purely for the enjoyment of the sport and competing against others. There are often no officials to enforce the rules in amateur games of basketball or tennis. If a team you played with or against for fun did not follow the ethics of sportsmanship, you would stop playing against them.

Finally, as we have seen, the values we develop through sportsmanship are essential for life. Of course, some people we meet in life set out to "win" at all costs, without showing respect for others. Fortunately, most people recognize the importance of fair play, teamwork, and doing the right thing. Whether these people are athletes or not, they recognize the values of sportsmanship.

TOPICS FOR DISCUSSION

As this book shows, there are many arguments and views about the meaning and importance of sportsmanship, and whether this is beneficial for sport.

Here are a few questions to consider:

- What do you think sportsmanship is? List some examples of good and bad sportsmanship that you have seen either in professional or amateur sport. Think about what qualities were shown by the athletes involved.

- Is winning more important than sportsmanship? If you play sport or support a team, what matters to you most? Would you be happy for your team to win unfairly? The team might not have deliberately or even knowingly gained an unfair advantage. Would you be prepared to lose an important game by doing the right thing?

- Are there times when showing sportsmanship is not the right thing to do? What if a team player gives an advantage to the opposition with a sportsmanlike gesture? Is this letting down the rest of the team or the fans? Your team might be playing a team that has not shown sportsmanlike behaviour – should you be sportsmanlike towards this team?

- Is it ever right to disagree with an official? We have seen examples in this book of players trying to correct an incorrect decision, not always successfully. If you know a decision to be wrong, should you try to correct it? Or should you always accept the decision?

- What role do you think coaches should play in encouraging sportsmanship? Is a coach's job to create a winning team, or a team that behaves in the right way? Do coaches always put sportsmanship ahead of a winning result?

- Do athletes have a responsibility to be good role models? Is this just about their behaviour in public, or on the field of play? Do athletes also have a responsibility to set a good example in their private lives? Compare athletes to other people whom we expect to behave well.

- Is sportsmanship dead? Many of the best examples of sportsmanship happened many years ago. Do you think people cared more about sportsmanship in the past? Does sportsmanship still have a place in modern sport, or is it an outdated concept? You could also look for more examples of bad sportsmanship in the past.

- What would happen if there were no sportsmanship? Imagine your favourite sport if every athlete believed in winning at all costs. Would the sport be very different? Would it be enjoyable to watch, or would people find another form of entertainment?

- Can you think of ways that ideas of sportsmanship can be applied outside sport? Is fair play more or less important in real life than it is in sport? What are the effects of bad sportsmanship on situations and people in the real world?

GLOSSARY

amateur someone who is not paid for doing something – for example, for playing a sport

arrogant overbearing and believing oneself to be better than other people

Aryan according to the beliefs of Adolf Hitler and the Nazis who ruled Germany in the 1930s and 1940s, a race of white, non-Jewish people

bias prejudice in favour of one side or the other in an argument

boycott refuse to attend something or deal with another group – for example, for political reasons

bribery when money or a gift is given to persuade someone to do something or help the giver, often illegally

chivalry code of honour developed by knights in medieval times

cold war period of tension from 1945 until around 1989 between two groups of countries led by the United States and the Soviet Union. Although the cold war included many conflicts, such as the Vietnam and Korean Wars, it was "cold" because there was no open conflict between the two groups.

colonial relating to a colony, which is a country or piece of land that is ruled by another country

commiserate to express pity or sympathy for someone

communist supporter of communism, which states that all property should be controlled by the government, with everyone working for the state. There were communist governments in much of Eastern Europe, the Soviet Union, and China during the second half of the 20th century.

controversial something about which people disagree or have different opinions

cultural shared values and lifestyle characteristics of a society

democracy society or organization that is controlled by the people it governs, by voting in elections

ethical relating to ethics, or issues of right and wrong

ethics issues of right and wrong

gamesmanship attempting to gain a psychological advantage over an opponent

graciousness showing modesty and courteousness

grassroots ordinary people, such as the many people who play a sport below the elite level

intimidate use aggressive behaviour to frighten or gain an advantage over someone

league group of sports teams that play against one another on a regular basis to determine which is the best

media collective name for different means of communication, such as newspapers, television, and the Internet

medieval relating to the Middle Ages, which lasted from the end of the Roman Empire until the 1400s

moral ethical, concerned with good or bad behaviour

performance-enhancing drug substance that athletes take in the belief that it will improve their performance. Steroids are an example of performance-enhancing drugs.

prejudice bias, being against or in favour of something

principle general rule followed by a person or thing

professional person who earns money for doing something – for example, for playing a sport

psychology study of how the mind works

racist someone who discriminates against people because of where they come from or the colour of their skin

sadistic enjoying inflicting pain on others

sledging insulting or verbally abusing an opponent

Soviet linked to the Soviet Union

Soviet Union country that existed from 1922 to 1991, made up of Russia and 14 other republics including Ukraine and Kazakhstan, which are all now separate countries

sportsmanship behaving in an honourable and sporting way while playing sport; fair play

steroids kind of drug taken by some athletes to improve their performance

truce agreement to temporarily stop war or conflict

NOTES ON SOURCES

SPORTSMANSHIP AND ETHICS (pages 4–5)
1. Craig Clifford and Randolph M. Feezell, *Sport and Character* (Human Kinetics, 2010), 10.

WHAT IS SPORTSMANSHIP? (pp 6–9)
1. Ronald B. Woods, *Social Issues in Sport* (Human Kinetics, 2007), 170.
2. Encyclopædia Britannica, s.v. "Coubertin, Pierre, Baron de".
3. David Miller, *Athens to Athens: The Official History of the Olympic Games and the IOC* (Mainstream Publishing, 2003), 53.
4. Max Davidson, *It's Not the Winning that Counts* (Little Brown, 2009), 110–14; Miller, *Athens to Athens*, 99.
5. Wimbledon, http://aeltc2010.wimbledon.org/en_GB/about/guide/faq.html#general.

FAIR PLAY IN HISTORY (pages 10–15)
1. Donald G. Kyle, "Winning at Olympia", http://www.archaeology.org.
2. Davidson, *It's Not the Winning that Counts*, 49.
3. Encyclopædia Britannica, s.v. "Association Football".
4. Encyclopædia Britannica, s.v. "Baseball".
5. John Major, *More Than a Game: The Story of Cricket's Early Years* (Harper Perennial, 2008), 341; Matthew Engel, "The Legacy of Grace", ESPN, 19 December 2009, http://www.espn-cricinfo.com/magazine/content/story/440091.html.
6. David Wallechinsky and Jaime Loucky, *The Complete Book of the Olympics* (Aurum Press, 2008), 31.
7. Miller, *Athens to Athens*, 61–63.
8. Ed Smith, *What Sport Tells Us About Life* (Penguin, 2008), 121.
9. George Orwell, "The Sporting Spirit", http://orwell.ru/library/articles/spirit/english/e_spirit.
10. BBC News, "Ryder Cup History: 1969", http://news.bbc.co.uk/sport1/hi/golf/3910485.stm.

RULES (pages 16–23)
1. Greg Couch, "Stealing Signs: Fair or Foul?" *Baseball Digest*, August 2002, http://findarticles.com/p/articles/mi_m0FCI/is_8_61/ai_88575166/.
2. Richard Williams, "Alberto Contador's chain reaction is Tour de France's defining moment", *The Guardian*, 20 July 2010, http://www.guardian.co.uk/sport/blog/2010/jul/20/albert-contador-tour-de-france.
3. BBC News, "Guide to Basketball", http://news.bbc.co.uk/sport1/hi/other_sports/basketball/4185400.stm.
4. Andrew Benson, "Schumacher's Chequered History", BBC News, 28 May 2006, http://news.bbc.co.uk/sport1/hi/motorsport/formula_one/5024532.stm.
5. Davidson, *It's Not the Winning that Counts*, 58–66.
6. Huffington Post, "Desota County High School Basketball Player Attacks Referee", 14 December 2010, http://www.huffingtonpost.com/2010/12/14/desoto-player-attacks-referee_n_796560.html?ref=email_share.

7. Lawrence Donegan, "Serena Williams Is Fined $10,500 for US Open Line Judge Tirade", *The Guardian*, 14 September 2009, http://www.guardian.co.uk/sport/2009/sep/13/serena-williams-tirade-us-open.
8. Gibson, Owen, "World Cup 2010: Stubborn Fifa rules out using goal-line technology", *The Guardian*, 28 June 2010, http://www.guardian.co.uk/football/2010/jun/28/world-cup-2010-goal-line-technology-fifa.
9. Bill Shaikin, "Baseball's blown calls renew instant replay debate", *Los Angeles Times*, 8 October 2010, http://articles.latimes.com/2010/oct/08/sports/la-spw-braves-giants-replay-20101009.
10. Smith, *What Sport Tells Us About Life*, 123.

RESPECT (pages 24–35)

1. Smith, *What Sport Tells Us About Life*, 120.
2. Larry Schwartz, "He Was a Pain . . . But a Great Pain", ESPN, http://espn.go.com/sportscentury/features/00014142.html.
3. Davidson, *It's Not the Winning that Counts*, 96–100.
4. Brian Goff, "Faking=Cheating? The Curious Case of Derek Jeter", *The Christian Science Monitor*, 21 September 2010, http://www.csmonitor.com/Business/The-Sports-Economist/2010/0921/Faking-cheating-The-curious-case-of-Derek-Jeter.
5. Paul Kelso, "Bloodgate: European Rugby Cup's Damning Judgment", *The Telegraph*, 26 August 2009, http://www.telegraph.co.uk/sport/rugbyunion/club/6089556/Bloodgate-European-Rugby-Cups-damning-judgment.html.
6. Davidson, *It's Not the Winning that Counts*, 244.
7. Ben Knight, "Michael Johnson: Olympic relay gold medal from Sydney Olympic Games is tainted", *The Daily Telegraph*, 3 June 2008.
8. Michael Johnson, "Why Drugs Cheat Shamed Me into Handing Back Olympic Relay Gold Medal", *The Telegraph*, 3 June 2008, http://www.telegraph.co.uk/sport/othersports/olympics/2302250/Michael-Johnson-Why-drugs-cheat-shamed-me-into-handing-back-Olympic-relay-gold-medal.html.
9. Associated Press, "Agassi: Book Part of Atonement for Lies", ESPN, 9 November 2009, http://sports.espn.go.com/sports/tennis/news/story?id=4636196.
10. WWE.com, http://www.wwe.com.
11. Davidson, *It's Not the Winning that Counts*, 119–124.
12. Davidson, *It's Not the Winning that Counts*, 93–97.
13. *Newsweek*, "I'm Not a Role Model", 28 June 1993, http://www.newsweek.com/1993/06/27/i-m-not-a-role-model.html.
14. *Newsweek*, "I'm Not a Role Model".

PRESSURE TO SUCCEED (pages 36–39)

1. Graham Hays, "Central Washington Offers the Ultimate Act of Sportsmanship", ESPN, 28 April 2008, http://sports.espn.go.com/ncaa/columns/story?columnist=hays_graham&id=3372631.

SPORTSMANSHIP AND CULTURE (pages 40–45)

1. Wallechinsky and Loucky, *The Complete Book of the Olympics*, 230–32.
2. Davidson, *It's Not the Winning that Counts*, 67–68.
3. Davidson, *It's Not the Winning that Counts*, 68.
4. Wallechinsky and Loucky, The Complete Book of the Olympics, 220.
5. Wallechinsky and Loucky, *The Complete Book of the Olympics*, 219–20.
6. Davidson, *It's Not the Winning that Counts*, 115–18.
7. Justin McCurry, "Sumo Wrestlers Admit Fixing Matches", *The Guardian*, 3 February 2011, http://www.guardian.co.uk/world/2011/feb/03/sumo-wrestlers-admit-fixing-matches.
8. Miller, *Athens to Athens*, 50.
9. Davidson, *It's Not the Winning that Counts*, 182–84.

SPORTSMANSHIP AND YOU (pages 46–49)

1. Josephson Institute, "What Are Your Children Learning? The Impact of High School Sports on the Values and Ethics of High School Athletes", 2007, http://josephsoninstitute.org/pdf/sports_survey_report_022107.pdf.
2. Josephson Institute, "What Are Your Children Learning?"
3. Josephson Institute, "What Are Your Children Learning?"
4. Davidson, *It's Not the Winning that Counts*, 226–29.
5. Davidson, *It's Not the Winning that Counts*, 228.
6. Josephson Institute, "What Are Your Children Learning?"
7. Petegoss.com, "Vendée Globe 1996/7", http://www.petegoss.com/journey-to-date-vendee-globe.php.

DOES SPORTSMANSHIP MATTER? (pages 50–53)

1. Richard Williams, "Old Man Rogge Should Hold His Tongue over Bolt", *The Guardian*, 21 August 2008, http://www.guardian.co.uk/sport/2008/aug/21/olympics2008.olympicsathletics4.
2. Associated Press, "Amid the Grieving, A Rare Act of Sportsmanship", Rivals.com, 18 February 2009, http://highschool.rivals.com/content.asp?CID=914609.

FIND OUT MORE

Books

Inside the Olympics, Nick Hunter (Raintree, 2012)
Respect Others, Respect Yourself (Life Skills), Sarah Medina (Raintree, 2009)
Rules of the Game (Football Focus), Clive Gifford (Wayland, 2009)
Sporting Success (British Issues), Jim Kerr (Franklin Watts, 2007)
Sports (Media Power), Jim Kerr (Franklin Watts, 2009)

Websites

Some of the best places to find examples of good and bad sportsmanship are news websites. They report the latest stories and often include articles describing the best and worst acts of sportsmanship. When looking at reports about sportsmanship on news websites, look out for bias. For example, if the article is talking about a decline in standards of sportsmanship, think about whether the writer is presenting a balanced view or a particular point of view.

www.fairplayinternational.org
Find out more about the International Fair Play Committee on this website. It is an international organization dedicated to the promotion of sportsmanship and fair play.

www.olympic.org/olympism in action
Sportsmanship has always been a big issue for the Olympic Movement, which aims to represent the best in sport. The International Olympic Committee's official website gives more details about how the Olympic Movement tries to promote values of excellence, friendship, and respect.

Many sports have their own campaigns around fair play and sportsmanship, such as the following:

www.fifa.com/aboutfifa/worldwideprograms/fifacampaigns/fairplay/ code.html
Football's world governing body FIFA seeks to promote fair play in the sport.

www.thefa.com/leagues/respect
The English Football Association runs a campaign to promote respect for officials and other players.

Places to visit

There is no single place you can visit to find out about sportsmanship, although many countries and sports have their own museums, such as the following:

Football
National Football Museum, Preston
www.nationalfootballmuseum.com

Scottish Football Museum, Glasgow
www.scottishfootballmuseum.org.uk

Cricket
MCC Museum, London
www.lords.org/history/mcc-museum

Rugby
World Rugby Museum, London
www.rfu.com/microsites/museum

Golf
British Golf Museum, St Andrews
www.britishgolfmuseum.co.uk

You can see examples of good and bad sportsmanship at any sporting event, whether you are watching top-level professional sport or your school or local team. Look at players and spectators and think about their attitudes towards sportsmanship.

- How are players treating the officials, such as the referee? Are they accepting decisions, or are they arguing with the officials?
- What is the attitude of spectators towards the opposing team, its fans, and the officials?
- How are the players behaving towards each other? Is the sport being played in the right spirit, or are the players trying to win at all costs, even if that means they are not playing fairly?

Write down your thoughts about sportsmanship at the game and ask others what they thought. Real examples and your own research are important parts of understanding a topic.

Suggestions for further research

There are a number of different ways to develop your knowledge of sportsmanship and related topics. Here are a few suggestions:

- This book has considered good and bad sportsmanship in a variety of sports, particularly the most high-profile team sports. Investigate standards of sportsmanship in your favourite sport. You might want to look at how the sport is played in different countries and whether there are different standards.
- Look in more detail at some of the pressures that professional athletes face, such as the role of money in sport. How does money affect your own favourite sport?
- Discover more about how the media deal with sportsmanship. Do media reports in newspapers and on websites encourage sportsmanship, or do they promote a win-at-all-costs mentality? Try to find examples of both sides of the argument.
- Look at examples of fairness in areas outside sport. Consider world issues such as poverty and trade. Are there areas in the real world where ideas of sportsmanship and fair play could make a big difference in people's lives?

INDEX

action replays 22, 23
Agassi, Andre 32
Ali, Muhammad 29
amateur athletes 13, 14, 53
American football 26, 28
apartheid 43

baseball 12, 17, 23, 24, 26, 30
basketball 18, 21, 26, 35, 47
Beckham, David 39
beliefs, standing up for 43
Berlin Olympics 42–43
biased attitudes 38
"bloodgate" scandal 27
Bolt, Usain 51
Bonds, Barry 30
boxing 28, 29
boycotts 43
bribery 11, 32

Caslavska, Vera 43
cheating 11, 30–31, 44, 46
chivalry 11
Cobb, Ty 24
Connors, Jimmy 33
Corinthians 20
Coubertin, Baron Pierre de 7
cricket 12, 13, 22, 25
cultural differences 40–41
cycling 18

Didrikson, Mildred "Babe" 9
disputed decisions 20, 21, 22–23
diving 26, 41, 48
drugs 30–31

ethical questions 5, 6

fair play 7, 10–11, 20, 36, 37, 41, 43, 46, 48
faking injury 26, 46
fans 14, 38

Federer, Roger 45
Flintoff, Andrew 25
football 4, 12, 16–17, 20, 23, 26, 40, 41
Formula One racing 19
fouls 18, 20
friendships 45

gamesmanship 12
gladiators 11
golf 13, 15, 50
Goss, Pete 49
Grace, W. G. 12
graciousness 6, 8, 9, 36, 37, 48
Greece, ancient 10–11

"hawkeye" systems 22
Henry, Thierry 16, 17
honesty 5, 8, 9, 47, 48
Hrbatý, Dominik 45

intimidation 24

Jacklin, Tony 15
Johnson, Michael 31
judo 41

Landy, John 33
leagues 13, 14
Long, Luz 42, 43

media coverage 14, 21

national pride 14–15, 38
Nicklaus, Jack 15

Olympic Games 7, 9, 10–11, 13, 14, 31, 42–43, 44, 51
origins of modern sport 12–13
Owens, Jesse 42–43

politics 42–43
pressures 36, 37, 38
professionalism, growth of 14
psychology 28

racism 42–43, 44
referees and umpires 8, 20, 21, 22, 26
respect 9, 24–25, 45
rivalries 14–15, 38
role models 34–35
rugby 6, 23, 27, 28
rules 4, 12, 16–23, 48, 51
Ryder Cup 15

school and college sports 13, 21, 37, 46, 47
Schumacher, Michael 19
Shiley, Jean 9
"sledging" 28
steroids 30
Stroud, Cleveland 47
sumo wrestling 44

technology 22–23
tennis 5, 22, 32, 33, 45
Thorpe, Jim 13
Tucholsky, Sara 37

unfair advantage 24, 26–28
unwritten rules 18

values for life 13, 48, 53
verbal abuse 28, 29

Williams, Serena 22, 34
Williams, Tom 27
win-at-all-costs mindset 9, 11, 24, 37, 46, 50, 53
World Cup 14, 16, 39
wrestling 10, 32, 44

Yamashita, Yasuhiro 41